CONTENTS

A frog starts life as a tiny egg.
In spring, a female frog lays the eggs in a pond.
The eggs are called frog spawn.

6

The female lays hundreds of eggs at a time, but some of them are eaten by birds and other frogs. The eggs look like little blobs of jelly, each with a tiny black dot inside. The eggs stick together in a big wobbly ball.

What are the black dots inside the blobs of jelly? Each dot is a tiny tadpole. Inside the eggs, the tadpoles grow bigger and bigger.

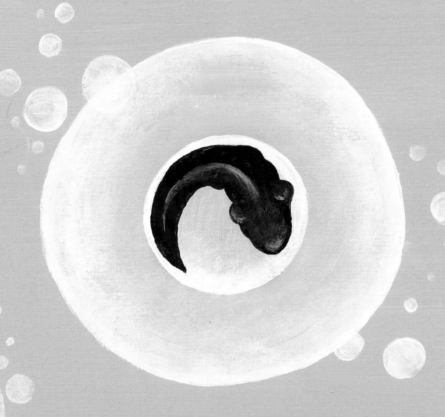

After about a month, the eggs start to hatch.

A squirming tadpole wiggles out of its
jelly ball. This tiny tadpole will grow into
a baby frog.

But the tadpole doesn't look like a frog yet.
It has a long, wiggly tail like a fish. It uses
its tail for swimming in the pond.

Every day, the tiny tadpole grows bigger and stronger. It feeds on plants growing in the water. It scrapes off pieces of the plants to eat.

When the tadpole
is six weeks old, it
grows two legs at the back.

Four weeks later, it grows
two legs at the front.

The tadpole still uses its
tail for swimming. But now it uses
its webbed feet as flippers, too.

The tadpole's tail becomes shorter and shorter until it's almost gone. At 12 weeks old, it doesn't look like a fish any more. It looks like a little frog!

The little frog is four months old. It climbs out of the water. It hops onto a plant stem growing by the water.

On land, the frog likes damp, dark places. During the day, it hides from animals that might gobble it up.

Animals such as birds, bats, and snakes like to eat frogs. When the frog is in danger, it dives back into the pond. Splash!

When the frog is hungry, it sits very still
and waits. Then it pokes out its long, sticky
tongue and gobbles up the insect!

A juicy worm makes another tasty treat for the frog. It's gone in one big gulp.

When it is three years old, the frog is grown up.
It goes back to the pond where it was born.
There, the male and female frogs mate. Then
the female frog lays her eggs in the water.

Soon the eggs will turn into tiny tadpoles.
And the tadpoles will turn into . . .

. . . lots of new little frogs!

Index

Further Information

The frogs featured in this book are common frogs (*Rana temporaria*). To find out more about them, visit:

www.arkive.org/species/ARK/amphibians/Rana_temporaria/